GERMANY

A panorama in color

90 color pictures

by leading German photographers

 Umschau Verlag Frankfurt am Main

English translation by John Dornberg, French translation by Emilie Müller-Bochat.
The introduction was adapted from an article by Rudolf Hagelstange.

10th edition 1973 · All rights reserved
Reproduction of the pictures only with the consent
of the photographers and the publisher
© 1962 Umschau Verlag Breidenstein KG, Frankfurt a. M.
Printed and bound by Brönners Druckerei Breidenstein KG, Frankfurt a. M.
ISBN 3-524-00039-8 · Printed in Germany

Colorful Germany

Each country has its own unique characteristics. Countries like Italy and Spain, for example, have common roots, but an observant visitor will recognize that they are vastly different. Ireland is so close to England, yet they are completely different in nature. Each land has its own history, culture, folklore, nature and landscape and these elements and forces combine to create something distinctive.

Germany, of course, is no exception, and for many years it has attracted visitors, not so much for its climate — such as the countries of the so-called sunny south — but for its varied scenic attractions. From the Alps in the south, to the coast of the North and Baltic seas, Germany presents such a magnificent panorama that even widely traveled Germans are still charmed and overwhelmed by out-of-the-way landscapes and districts they have not visited before.

Natural, architectural and cultural marvels, for instance, make southern Germany, between the Main River and the Alps, one of the richest and loveliest regions in the world. No mere listing or description will do justice to the beauty and variety of the landscape. Snow-capped mountains, wooded foothills, large cities, world-famous churches in idyllic surroundings, monuments of artistic achievement, centers of creative energy combine to characterize the region, so rich in natural wonders, history and culture that even its inhabitants often do not realize the wealth of their treasure. Other areas, moreover, as if to compensate for a certain lack of natural attractions, boast castles and towers of industry — such as the Ruhr Basin — which in their own way attract visitors and evoke their admiration.

A network of highways and rail or bus lines connects the largest cities with the smallest, most remote villages; the noisy turmoil of the metropolis with the idyllic rural regions; neon-illuminated boulevards with moonlit squares of medieval towns. Mighty rivers such as the Danube and the Rhine traverse the country to flow over its borders to neighboring lands and eventually spill into the sea. Smaller tributaries lace the country like a finely-spun web, flowing past lovely vine-covered hills until, in peaceful but determined fashion, they meander toward the major arteries. The rivers are an integral part of the German scene and have contributed extensively to its folklore.

Although the German Alps are but a modest part of that massive, craggy European range, the mountain regions in Germany's heartland — such as the Black Forest, the Harz, the Thuringian Forest or the Taunus range — have almost no match in other countries and are, in a way, symbolic of Germany. The Black Forest, for example, embodies all that a German forest with its lore of elves and witches represents to visitors from abroad. The Harz Mountains and the Thuringian woods are known to people even in faraway lands through the works of Goethe and Heine. The woods of Germany have always charmed foreigners and when Germans travel outside their country, it is always the lore and memory of the forests and woodlands that they take with them.

Germany is also rich in coastal lands, such as the moor regions of Eastern Frisia and off-shore islands like the Frisian chain, Sylt, Föhr, the Halligen and Rügen.

It is a country, too, of large cities like Hamburg, Bremen, Magdeburg, Lübeck, Cologne, Düsseldorf, Hanover, Mannheim, Stuttgart, Karlsruhe, Heidelberg, Nuremberg, Regensburg, Kiel, Flensburg, Trier, Aachen, Berlin and Munich, cities that have been influenced by the sea or by the rivers that flow through them.

The purpose of this book is to present a composite and representative view of this variegated country with its multitude of man-made and natural wonders. Because it is a book of color photographs, this proved to be a doubly difficult task, for it raised problems not only of selecting photographs that mirror the character of the country — such as the editors faced when they compiled a companion volume of black-and-white photos — but of choosing those views and scenes that would lend the finished product color and variety.

The collection of photos is meant to be an echo of the diversified character of Germany and, also, representative of the nature of the country. A view of one alpine meadow is illustrative of many; a picture of one mountain region, symbolic of others; a farm landscape, typical of numerous such scenes. The same is true for the abbeys and cathedrals, the castles and river valleys, the quaint, medieval villages of southern Germany and the great cities of the north. Decisive in the selection of each photograph was its power to interpret and represent similar regions nearby or elsewhere.

Another element entered into the selection process — the dimension of color. Substituting a color photograph for a black-and-white shot is simple enough, technically. But there is far more involved than merely the technical considerations. For, color is symbolic. It has a value

4

of its own, breathing temperament, exuding temperature and intensifying, deepening and multiplying what the eye perceives. Each color by itself evokes different feelings and brings different standards of taste and composition into play in a manner quite apart from the black--and-white photograph.

There are a number of pictures in this volume — for example, the view of the little church "Kappl" in the Upper Palatinate, the glittering neon lights in the view of the Kurfürstendamm in Berlin, or the glowing Rhön landscape — which remind you of romantic, realist, impressionist, or even, expressionist painters who used similar colors on canvas for the same scenes. This, of course, is not the purpose or goal of color photography. It serves merely as a standard of comparison. Color photography is a new form of seeing life and objects, one which will have to develop and follow its own artistic laws. Much of this will depend on the demands themselves which we place upon this new form — whether it will be allowed to degenerate into calendar art, or reach creative heights of its own.

A good color picture, of course, depends on more than merely the artistic abilities of the photographer. It is influenced by numerous external factors such as the weather, the lighting, the time of year, etc. Without a certain amount of luck, not even the most gifted photographer will be able to produce a good landscape shot. There is more, too, to this new art than merely the ability to recognize a good subject when the sky is blue and the sun bathes a beautiful scene in bright light. There is a great difference between what the eye sees and what the camera and film record, for the eye is a living organ that not only mirrors what it sees but reacts subjectively and *interprets*, subject to numerous influences and illusions, the scene before it. The camera, on the other hand, is a tool, subject to chemical and physical laws.

The photographs in this volume have been produced, for the most part, by a still small group of men who, on their trips and photographic expeditions, have tried not only to take shots that meet the highest technical standards of color photography, but to produce *pictures* that characterize a certain region or object. These are photographs that reflect the central theme of the book — Germany, portraying it in terms of its countryside, its large cities and little towns, its typical architecture. It is in a way a pictorial anthology of Germany.

List of Illustrations

6

7

Lake Chiemsee

The largest of the Bavarian lakes, the Chiemsee, is situated at the foot of the Alps, between Rosenheim and Traunstein. The small Frauen-insel, an island, is the site of a nunnery founded in the 9th century. A larger island, Herreninsel, boasts a 19th century castle.

Le lac Chiemsee

Au pied des Alpes, entre Rosenheim et Traunstein, s'étale le plus grand des lacs bavarois. La petite «île des femmes» (Fraueninsel) doit son nom à un couvent de femmes, du IXe siècle. La photo montre le lac sous un soleil de février.

The Reiteralpe

In the winter the Reiteralpe is a favorite skiing area. During the summer months when cattle graze on the lush green meadows, this easternmost part of the Bavarian Alps, near the resort town of Berchtesgaden, is besieged by mountain climbers.

La Reiteralpe

Ce plateau se trouve près de Berchtesgaden, dans la partie orientale des Alpes bavaroises. Les alpages, où broute pendant l'été le bétail venu des vallées, sont devenus de nos jours un paradis pour les skieurs.

Tegernsee

The numerous lakes at the foot of the Alps add to the charm and beauty of the Bavarian countryside that surrounds the city of Munich. View of the Tegernsee, with the village of Rottach-Egern and the Wallberg in the background.

Tegernsee

La Bavière, avec ses nombreux lacs au pied des Alpes, possède un parc national somptueux. Aux portes de Munich: Vue sur Rottach-Egern et le Wallberg, surplombant le lac Tegern.

Höglwörth

These buildings, situated among scenic, solitary Alpine foothills between Traunstein and Salzburg, once an Augustine abbey, are a fine example of Bavarian Rococo architecture.

Höglwörth

C'est une construction en rococo bavarois (XVIIe s.), située dans un paysage charmant et calme des contreforts alpestres, entre Traunstein et Salzbourg. C'était autrefois un cloître de chanoines augustins.

Garmisch-Partenkirchen

This fashionable international resort town is surrounded by craggy peaks and lies at the foot of the Zugspitze, Germany's highest mountain (10,000 ft.). Garmisch-Partenkirchen was the scene of the 1936 Winter Olympic Games.

Garmisch-Partenkirchen

Au pied du massif grandiose de la Zugspitze, montagne la plus haute d'Allemagne (2963 m), on découvre la vie mondaine d'une station climatique internationale ... et, tout près, le calme du monde alpestre.

THE WEISSENSEE IN THE ALLGÄU. View over
the rich pastures of the Allgäu,
famous for its cattle and dairy products,
with the Lechtal Alps rising in the back.
The town of Füssen is seen in the background.

LE WEISSENSEE DANS L'ALLGÄU. Au-delà des
riches prairies de l'Allgäu, connu pour
l'élevage du bétail, le regard s'étend
jusqu'aux Alpes de la vallée du Lech, à la
frontière tyrolienne.
Au fond, la ville de Füssen.

St. Koloman near Füssen

This simple, beautifully designed 18th century pilgrimage church with its onion-shaped dome is typical of many churches and chapels in scenic Bavaria. It is situated in the Allgäu region.

St Koloman, près de Füssen

Lieu de pélerinage, cette église du XVIIIe siècle, au style sobre et équilibré avec sa «tour oignon», sise au milieu d'un ravissant paysage, est le type caractéristique de nombre d'églises et de chapelles rustiques de la Bavière.

Munich

Bavaria's 800-year-old capital now has a population of more than one million. Towering over a mass of ancient roofs and modernistic buildings are the spires of the Frauenkirche (the Church of Our Lady), the Town-Hall, Saint Peter's and the Church of the Holy Ghost.

Munich

La vieille capitale de la Bavière, fondée il y a 800 ans, a aujourd'hui plus d'un million d'habitants. Au-dessus des maisons, vieilles et modernes, surgissent les tours de Notre-Dame, de Saint-Pierre, du Saint-Esprit, et de l'hôtel de ville.

The Church "In der Wies"

The Church in the Meadow, not far from Oberammergau, was built by Dominicus Zimmermann between 1745 and 1754. It is a gem among the many lavishly decorated baroque churches in Bavaria. Shown here is the upper portion of the choir.

L'église «In der Wies»

L'église «Dans les Prés», non loin d'Oberammergau, fut édifiée par Dominique Zimmermann entre 1745 et 54. C'est un joyau parmi les églises bavaroises, somptueuses de style baroque. Vue sur la partie supérieure du chœur, d'où émane une luminosité rayonnante.

Passau

Passau, at the confluence of the Danube, Inn and Ilz rivers, near the Austro-German border, has been an influential bishopric since the 8th century. Shown here is a vista of the Inn River promenade which has an almost Italian appearance.

Passau

Passau, ville frontière avec l'Autriche, située au confluent du Danube, de l'Inn et de l'Ilz, est un célèbre siège épiscopal depuis le huitième siècle. Vue sur la rive de l'Inn, rappelant presque l'Italie septentrionale.

Regensburg

The city on the Danube, shown here in an aerial photograph, was founded by the Celts 2,500 years ago. Its many medieval buildings and monuments testify to its long history. The cathedral was started in 1250 and completed in 1870.

Ratisbonne

Une fondation celtique, Ratisbonne sur le Danube, édifiée voici 2.500 ans, est encore riche en monuments du moyen âge. La cathédrale commencée en 1250, ne fut achevée qu'en 1870.

Weltenburg

An oval abbey church (1713-43) with a magnificent interior was built at this beautiful spot on the Danube, southwest of Regensburg, by Cosmas Damian Asam, a famous architect, painter and stucco artist of the 18th century.

Weltenbourg

L'emplacement de l'église conventuelle, dans la vallée du Danube au sud-ouest de Ratisbonne, est d'une beauté particulière. Edifiée par Cosmas Damian Asam, architecte, peintre et stucateur à la fois, cette église (1713-43) se distingue par sa forme ovale et sa décoration.

Augsburg

This proud old Imperial Town, the pulsating center of the Bavarian part of Swabia, is Bavaria's third-largest city with a population of 210,000. Shown here, next to the Perlach Tower, is the Town-Hall, built between 1610 and 1620 by Elias Holl. It is considered one of the finest examples of early German Baroque.

Augsbourg

L'hôtel de ville, centre de la vieille capitale de la Souabe bavaroise, s'élève près de la tour de Perlach. Bâti par Elias Holl en 1610-1620, c'est le premier monument du baroque allemand. Augsbourg reste de nos jours encore la troisième ville de Bavière (210000 h.) et un centre industriel important.

Ulm

Above the stately, old patrician houses on the banks of the Danube River rises the highest church spire of the world (528 feet). The Gothic Minster (1377-1890) is the pride of this former Imperial City.

Ulm

Au-dessus des maisons patriciennes qui longent la rive du Danube, s'élève le clocher le plus haut du monde (161 m). La cathédrale gothique (1377-1890) est la gloire de cette ancienne «ville libre».

34

The Upper Danube Valley

The Danube, when it is still young, cuts deeply into the Swabian Jura mountains between Tuttlingen and Sigmaringen. The river here flows through many deep canyons. View from Werenwag Castle.

La vallée du Danube supérieur

Entre Tuttlingen et Sigmaringen, le Danube pénètre profondément dans le Jura Souabe. Des falaises bordent le fleuve tout juste encore un jeune ruisseau. Vue du château fort Werenwag.

Lake Constance

Also called "The Swabian Sea", Lake Constance, bordered by Germany, Switzerland and Austria, is one of the largest lakes in Europe (204 square miles). Shown here is a view from the Pfänder Mountain toward the island city of Lindau.

Le lac de Constance

Le lac de Constance, où convergent l'Allemagne, la Suisse et l'Autriche, est l'un des plus grands lacs d'Europe (538 km²). Du mont Pfänder, le regard glisse sur l'île de Lindau.

Meersburg

Meersburg, known for cozy little wine taverns, picturesque narrow streets and an age-old castle, is a popular tourist town on Lake Constance. The castle (shown here) has remained unaltered since the 16th century.

Meersbourg

Cette petite ville sur le lac de Constance, avec ses ruelles et ses tavernes sympathiques, est très fréquentée des touristes. Le vieux château, tel qu'il se présente aujourd'hui, date du XVIe siècle.

Säckingen

A romantic small town with a long history, Säckingen lies in the scenic region of the Upper Rhine near the Swiss border. Shown here are its medieval wooden bridge (15th century) and the minster, founded in the 6th century by Saint Fridolin.

Säckingen

La ville est située dans le charmant paysage du haut Rhin, proche de la frontière suisse. Le pont de bois moyenâgeux et la cathédrale que Saint Fridolin a fondée au VIe siècle, en sont les caractéristiques.

Freiburg in the Breisgau

Freiburg is the gate to the Black Forest and a famous university town. Gaily colored market stalls dot the square at the foot of the Gothic Minster, in front of the Renaissance colonnade of the "Old Merchants' Hall" (built in 1532 by Lienhard Müller).

Fribourg-en-Brisgau

Fribourg, porte ouverte sur la Forêt-Noire, possède une université célèbre. Son beau «Vieux Magasin» (bâti en 1532), sur la place du marché, se voit au pied de la cathédrale gothique.

The Black Forest

Deep, dark woods and wide, open meadows characterize the huge forest that stretches from the Upper Rhine almost to Lake Constance. In our picture, the Bärental (Bear Valley).

La Forêt-Noire

Entre le haut Rhin et le lac de Constance, s'échelonnent les montagnes de la Forêt-Noire, sur une longueur de 158 km. D'immenses forêts y alternent avec de vastes prairies. Sur la photo: la «vallée des ours» (Bärental), près du Feldberg.

The Feldberg

This is the highest mountain of the Black Forest and all of south-west Germany, with an elevation of nearly 5,000 feet. It dominates the surrounding forest land and is the center of a popular winter sports region as well as a summer resort area.

Le Feldberg

Le Feldberg (1493 m) est le point culminant de la Forêt-Noire dans le sud-ouest de l'Allemagne. C'est en même temps le centre d'une région de sports d'hiver enchanteresse.

Altensteig

This small and friendly town in the Nagold Valley, north of Freuden-stadt, is a charming Black Forest resort that has carefully preserved its colorful old houses.

Altenstei⌐

L'une de ces petites villes de la Forêt-Noire, dans la vallée de la Nagold, où l'on tient amoureusement à l'architecture traditionnelle, avec ses faîtes caractéristiques et ses couleurs riantes.

Stuttgart

The capital of Baden-Württemberg has about 640,000 inhabitants and is the home of leading industries that have gravitated around the old city's center. Shown here are the market square with the Schiller monument, the city hall and the Late Gothic Stiftskirche.

Stuttgart

La capitale du Bade-Wurtemberg a environ 640.000 habitants. On y trouve des industries de réputation mondiale, établies autour du vieux centre: le marché avec le monument de Schiller, l'hôtel de ville et la Stiftskirche, de style gothique.

Hoher Rechberg

The Swabian Jura, a range of hills known for their rather rough climate, runs from south-west to north-east through most of Württemberg. Shown is a view of the "Hoher Rechberg" (left in the picture) near the town of Schwäbisch Gmünd.

Hoher Rechberg

Le Jura Souabe est une chaîne de hauteur moyenne, s'allongeant du S.-O. au N.-E. à travers le Wurtemberg. C'est un paysage agréable, mais de climat souvent assez rude. Vue sur le mont «Hoher Rechberg», près de Schwäbisch Gmünd.

Schwäbisch Hall

Schwäbisch Hall used to be a center of salt mining. Today it is a mineral spa. The old town, located on the banks of the Kocher River, has preserved its medieval appearance. Romanesque-Gothic St. Michael's Church is one of its major points of interest.

Schwäbisch Hall

Jadis centre de saliculture, Schwäbisch Hall est aujourd'hui une ville d'eau (eaux salines). Sur la rive du Kocher, la ville déploie son architecture médiévale intacte, dont l'église Saint-Michel, de style roman-gothique, est un exemple frappant.

Weissenburg in Bavaria

The tower of the Ellingen Gate, one of the most majestic city gates in Germany, dates to the 14th century, its outer part to 1520. In the background, the tower of St. Andrew's Church.

Weissenbourg, en Bavière

La tour de l'«Ellinger Tor», une des portes les plus imposantes en Allemagne, est du XIVe siècle; l'avant-corps est de 1520. Au fond: le clocher de l'église Saint-André.

Rothenburg on the Tauber

Rothenburg's medieval appearance has remained untouched by the passage of time. This charming old town is still entirely surrounded by its original defensive wall. Shown here are two of the romantic city-towers.

Rothenbourg-sur-le-Tauber

A l'intérieur de ses murailles, cette ville unique a parfaitement conservé son caractère moyenâgeux. Vue sur les tours romantiques de la ville.

Nuremberg

The city of the Master Singers and the home of Albrecht Dürer, Nuremberg was one of the richest and most influential of the old Imperial Cities. View of the Wasserturm (Water Tower, 1320-25) and Henkersteg (Hangman's Bridge, 13th century) and the 15th century Weinstadel (Wine Storage House).

Nuremberg

La ville des Maîtres-Chanteurs et d'Albert Durer, fut une des plus riches parmi les villes libres au moyen âge. Vue sur le Wasserturm (château d'eau, 1320-25) et le Henkersteg (XIIIe s.), et sur le dépôt de vins («Weinstadel»; XVe siècle).

In the Upper Palatinate

This little church, built in 1689 and dedicated to the Trinity, lies in the hilly, wooded Upper Palatinate region, north of the "Bavarian Forest", near the town of Waldsassen. It is called "Kappl".

Dans le Haut-Palatinat

Dans la région montueuse et boisée du nord de la Forêt Bavaroise, on trouve cette petite église, dite «Kappl», située non loin de Waldsassen, dans un paysage dégagé. Construite en 1689, elle est consacrée à la Trinité.

The Fichtel Mountains

Ochsenkopf peak, capped by a television transmitter, towers more than 3,400 feet over the woods and cliffs of the Fichtel region north of Bayreuth. Germany's famous porcelain industry is located in this area.

Dans les montagnes Fichtel

La «tête de bœuf» (Ochsenkopf), avec son poste émetteur de télévision, s'élève jusqu'à une altitude de 1024 m, au-dessus des forêts et des rochers du «Fichtelgebirge», au nord de Bayreuth. Grâce aux richesses du sol, cette région est un centre de l'industrie de porcelaine allemande.

Coburg

In Upper Fronconia not far from the "East Zone" border, lies the town of Coburg and its famous fortress. Its former ducal rulers are interrelated with many of Europe's royal houses. Ahorn Castle is shown in the foreground, with Coburg Fortress visible on the horizon.

Cobourg

En Haute-Franconie, près du «rideau de fer»: la ville et le château fort de Cobourg. La famille ducale portant ce nom, est liée à nombre de maisons d'Europe. Au premier plan, le château d'Ahorn; au fond, celui de Cobourg.

Bamberg

The historic structures and artistic treasures of this Franconian bishopric have remained unharmed through the centuries. The Romanesque cathedral (finished c. 1250), which contains beautifully sculpted
figures, dominates the town on the Regnitz River.

Bamberg

La ville, important siège épiscopal en Franconie, a pu garder intacts
ses belles œuvres d'architecture et ses trésors artistiques. La cathédrale romane (achevée vers 1250) avec ses vénérables sculptures, est
le cœur de cette ville sur la Regnitz.

SULZFELD, southeast of Würzburg,
is an old Franconian town, famous
for its wines. Adjacent to the city gate,
one can see the decorative gable of
the early Baroque town-hall.

SULZFELD, au sud-est de Wurtzbourg,
l'un de ces vieux villages sur le Main,
en Franconie, où l'on cultive aussi
la vigne. A côté de la porte, le fronton
splendide de l'hôtel de ville de
style baroque.

Würzburg

Würzburg, an old bishopric and university city in Franconia, lies on the Main River at the foot of a mighty fortress, surrounded by vine-covered hills. Our picture shows a view over the Main bridge to the Romanesque Cathedral (in the center).

Wurzbourg

Wurzbourg en Franconie est un siège épiscopal et une ville universitaire de vieux renom; elle est située au pied d'une forteresse et environnée de vignes. Vue sur le pont du Mein et sur la cathédrale, de style roman (au centre de la photo).

75

Miltenberg

This picturesque old town lies south of Aschaffenburg on the Main River. The "Riese", or Giant, one of Germany's oldest inns, is located here. Magnificent half-timbered houses line the streets.

Miltenberg

Miltenberg sur le Mein est située au sud d'Aschaffenbourg. On trouve ici le «Riese», l'une des plus anciennes auberges d'Allemagne, ainsi que nombre de beaux bâtiments caractéristiques.

Mespelbrunn

Hidden in the solitary Spessart Forest between Frankfurt and Würzburg, this 16th century palace is the perfect example of a romantic, moated castle and attracts numerous visitors.

Mespelbrunn

Ce château, entre Francfort-sur-le-Mein et Wurzbourg, est resté longtemps caché dans les forêts du Spessart; de nos jours, il est très recherché en tant que «château d'eau» romantique tout à fait typique. L'architecture, telle qu'elle se présente actuellement, est du XVIe siècle.

In the Rhön Mountains

The Rhön region, bordered by Hesse, Thuringia and Bavaria, is marked by numerous volcanic basalt cones. One of its most striking peaks is the Milseburg (c. 2,700 feet).

Dans les montagnes de la Rhön

Des monts coniques, en basalte et d'origine volcanique, caractérisent ce paysage, dans la Hesse, où confinent la Thuringe et la Bavière. La Milsebourg (835 m) est l'une des plus belles montagnes de la région.

Michelstadt

This town, situated in the wooded mountain region of the Odenwald, is known for its 15th century, half-timbered city hall (1484), one of the most beautiful in Germany. It is easily recognized by its three little spires and wooden columns. Behind it is St. Michael's Church (erected from 1461 to 1537).

Michelstadt

Michelstadt est situé dans la Forêt de l'Oden. Son hôtel de ville, construit en 1484, est parmi les plus beaux d'Allemagne: sur le vestibule ouvert se pose un étage d'un riche colombage, couronné de trois petites tours. Au fond, l'église Saint-Michel (1461-1537).

Heidelberg

Heidelberg with its famous university (founded in 1386), is one of the romantic showpieces among Germany's old towns. Its castle was built in Renaissance forms in the 16th century and ruined in 1689 and 1693. The Neckar River, shown in our picture, flows into the Rhine not far from Heidelberg.

Heidelberg

Heidelberg sur le Neckar, avec son université fondée en 1386, est une des villes les plus pittoresques d'Allemagne. Son château fut bâti au XVIe siècle et détruit en 1689 et 1693.

The Neckar

The Neckar is one of Germany's most romantic rivers. Numerous old castles and fortresses overlook the winding stream as it cuts through the Odenwald near Heidelberg. In the background, Hirschhorn Castle with its Romanesque tower and 16th century palace.

Le Neckar

Cette rivière, traversant tortueusement la Forêt de l'Oden près de Heidelberg, est bordée de nombreux châteaux forts. Au fond, le château fort Hirschhorn avec sa tour romane; l'hôtel seigneurial est du XVIe siècle.

Mannheim

With its extensive docks on the Rhine and the Neckar, which now deal with 30,000 ships a year, with its highly developed industry, and its population of 330,000, Mannheim has become a commercial center of economic importance. The former royal Residence, in its famous chequer-board layout, was built in the 17th century for the Elector Karl Theodor von der Pfalz. The picture shows the western approach to the Rhine bridge, which connects the town with Ludwigshafen.

Mannheim

Avec ses vastes installations portuaires sur le Rhin et le Neckar, où passent 30 000 bateaux par an, et son industrie très développée, Mannheim est devenu un centre de gravité économique, de 330 000 habitants. La résidence du Prince Electeur Karl Theodor a été construite en damier au XVIIe s. Photo: sortie ouest vers le pont du Rhin, qui conduit à Ludwigshafen.

88

Mainz

The cathedral, dedicated in 1009 and rebuilt in the Romanesque style, reigns over this 2,000-year-old city at the confluence of the Rhine and Main rivers. Since 1947, Mainz has been the capital of the Rhineland-Palatinate. After the last war, a university was founded here.

Mayence

Mayence est une ville édifiée voici 2.000 ans, située au confluent du Rhin et du Mein, que domine la cathédrale aux nombreuses tours, consacrée en 1009. Depuis 1947, Mayence est la capitale de Rhénanie-Palatinat.

Worms

In the 5th century, this ancient city on the Rhine was the capital of Burgundy. It is also the scene of the Nibelungen Saga. The Late Romanesque cathedral, completed c. 1240, has been preserved intact. View of the west choir.

Worms

La cathédrale impériale, de style roman (achevée vers 1240), domine cette ville sur le Rhin, qui au Ve siècle fut la capitale de la Burgundie, pays des «Nibelungen».

Frankfurt on the Main

This city, the birthplace of Goethe (1749), is an important trade and communications center, a tradition that goes back to the great fairs of the Middle Ages. The Gothic cathedral dates from the 13th and 14th centuries. In former times it was the scene of the coronations of the German emperors.

Francfort-sur-le-Mein

Francfort, connu pour ses foires depuis le moyen âge, est, aussi de nos jours, une importante ville commerciale. C'est la ville natale de Goethe (1749). La cathédrale gothique date du XIIIe et XIVe s.

Limburg

Limburg is situated on the Lahn River which flows into the Rhine south of Coblence. The valley is known for its many castles, churches and fortresses. Limburg's Romanesque-Gothic cathedral with its seven spires was completed in 1235.

Limbourg

La vallée de la Lahn, qui rejoint le Rhin au sud de Coblence, est riche en châteaux et en églises. La cathédrale de Limbourg fut achevée en 1235, dans un style romano-gothique.

The Argenstein Mill

This old watermill in the Lahn Valley, not far from Marburg, could have figured in the fairy tales of the Grimm brothers who collected many of their stories in Hesse. Picturesque, half-timbered houses characterize these villages.

Le moulin d'Argenstein

Dans la vallée de la Lahn, à proximité de Marbourg, le moulin d'Argenstein nous rapelle que, dans la Hesse précisément, les frères Grimm ont recueilli leurs contes populaires. Le joli colombage des maisons donne un cachet original à ces villages.

Bacharach on the Rhine

This ancient small town, characteristic of the middle Rhine, is nestled among vineyards. The romantic ruin of the Gothic Werner Chapel stands adjacent to the 13th century Saint Peter's Church. The view here is upstream toward Lorch.

Bacharach-sur-le-Rhin

La ville ancienne est environnée de vignobles célèbres. A côté de l'église Saint-Pierre (XIIIe siècle), se trouvent les vestiges de la chapelle de Werner, de style gothique. Vue en amont, vers Lorch.

Völklingen

Situated on the Saar River, Völklingen, a very old town, is one of the centers of German heavy industry. It is surrounded not only by pit heaps but by pleasant wooded hills.

Völklingen

Cette vieille ville sur la Sarre, l'un des centres de l'industrie lourde allemande, est entourée non seulement de hautes haldes, mais aussi de collines agréablement boisées.

Trier

The Porta Nigra, or Black Gate, built probably in the 4th century A. D., is the most magnificent relic of Roman rule on German soil. It was the city gate to ancient Augusta Treverorum, the "Rome of the North", on the Moselle River.

Trèves

Trèves, sur la Moselle, est une ancienne résidence impériale des Romains. La «Porta Nigra» est le plus beau monument de cette époque existant sur le sol allemand. La ville renferme en plus d'autres ruines importantes (IIIe et IVe s.).

Eltz Castle

This picturesque, ancient stronghold, situated near Moselkern in a solitary valley off the Moselle River, looks as if it had been transplanted from medieval times to the present. It has been in the possession of one and the same family of counts since 1150.

Le Château d'Eltz

Près de Moselkern, ce château est situé dans une vallée solitaire un peu éloignée de la Moselle. Il appartient à la même famille de comtes depuis 1150. L'architecture fait penser à l'époque de la Table ronde.

The Moselle

Winding and twisting its way toward Coblence, the Moselle, just as its big brother, the Rhine, is known for its superb white wines. Beilstein, a typical wine village on the romantic river, is shown here.

La Moselle

Décrivant d'innombrables méandres avant de rejoindre le Rhin, à Coblence, la Moselle a un vin blanc aussi réputé que celui du Rhin. Beilstein, sur notre photo, est un village typique de vignerons.

Bonn

Bonn, known formerly only as a pleasant university town on the Rhine and as Beethoven's birthplace, has been the provisional capital of the German Federal Republic since 1949. Our picture shows the district around the Bundeshaus, West Germany's house of parliament.

Bonn

Bonn sur le Rhin, connu autrefois surtout pour son université et pour être la ville natale de Beethoven, est aujourd'hui la capitale provisoire de la République Fédérale. La photo montre le Parlement et ses environs.

Aachen

The cathedral at Aachen, or Aix-la-Chapelle, dates to the 9th century. The Gothic choir (shown in the picture) was added to the church of Charlemagne in 1355. Beneath the "Double Madonna" (1524) is the Shrine of Charlemagne (1215) and the Golden Altar (1020).

Aix-la-Chapelle

Le chœur gothique fut ajouté, en 1355, à la chapelle de Charlemagne (consacrée en 805). Au-dessous de la Madone (1524): la châsse de Charlemagne (1215) et l'autel en or (1020).

Cologne

View of the cathedral over the Rhine River, with the Hohenzollern Bridge. Cologne's majestic cathedral was built over a period of six centuries, from 1248 to 1880. Third-largest city in Western Germany, Cologne has a population of 810,000.

Cologne

Vue sur le Rhin, avec le pont Hohenzollern. Dans cette ville, la troisième d'Allemagne occidentale, vivent 810.000 habitants. La cathédrale, commencée en 1248, ne fut achevée qu'en 1880.

Düsseldorf

The Thyssen Building, on Jan Wellem Platz, is one of the landmarks of this metropolis. Düsseldorf, with its 700,000 population, is the administrative center of the Rhineland-Westphalian industrial region. It has a special reputation for elegance.

Düsseldorf

Le gratte-ciel Thyssen, sur la place Jan Wellem, dans la métropole de l'industrie de Rhénanie-Westphalie. Düsseldorf est aussi une ville très élégante, de 700.000 habitants.

In the Ruhr District

Duisburg, near the confluence of the Rhine and Ruhr rivers, is an important center in that vast agglomeration of heavy industry which has made the name of a relatively small river, the Ruhr, known all over the world. Shown here are the Phoenix-Rheinrohr smelterworks in Duisburg-Ruhrort, with the Rhine barely visible in the background.

A la Ruhr

Près du confluent du Rhin et de la Ruhr se trouve Duisbourg, l'un des principaux centres de l'immense région industrielle qui a rendu célèbre le nom d'une modeste rivière. Vue sur les usines sidérurgiques Phoenix-Rheinrohr, à Duisbourg-Ruhrort.

Essen

Lake Baldeney was formed as a water reservoir in the Ruhr Valley in 1933. Today it is a favorite Ruhr area resort center. Shown in the foreground is Villa Hügel, at one time the residence of the Krupp family. The park surrounding the villa is now open to the public.

Essen

Le «lac Baldeney», achevé en 1933 pour servir de réservoir d'eau dans la vallée de la Ruhr, est devenu un lieu de villégiature de cette région industrielle. On voit, au premier plan, la «Villa Hügel», ancienne demeure de la famille Krupp.

Dortmund

This old Hanseatic town which has 640,000 inhabitants today, is the largest city in Westphalia and a center of heavy industry. The Westfalenhalle, shown in our picture, is an auditorium seating 25,000. It is surrounded by parks and sports fields and used for athletic and various cultural events such as concerts.

Dortmund

La plus grande ville de la Westphalie, avec ses 640.000 habitants, est un centre de l'industrie lourde. Jardins et établissements de sport contribuent au divertissement de la population, aussi bien que la «Westfalenhalle», bâtie en 1952 pour des manifestations sportives et culturelles, et pouvant recevoir 25.000 personnes environ.

Wilhelmshöhe near Kassel

This park was created in the 18th century by an Italian, Giovanni Francesco Guerniero, for a landgrave of Hesse. At its highest point rises a statue of Hercules (by Johann Jakob Anthony, 1713-1717) who reigns over a "Castle of the Giants" and a magnificent waterfall.

Wilhelmshöhe, près de Cassel

Sur l'obélisque de 30 m, s'élève l'imposante statue d'Hercule au-dessus du «château des géants» et de la cascade, dans le parc créé au XVIIIe siècle pour un landgrave de Hesse.

124

The Weser Valley

The Weser River flows into the North Sea near Bremen. Its upper region is one of Germany's most pleasant river landscapes and perfect for boat trips. Shown here is the valley near Steinmühle.

La vallée du Weser

Le Weser qui débouche au nord de Brême dans la mer du Nord, forme dans son cours moyen l'un des plus jolis paysages de rivière d'Allemagne; un vrai paradis pour le canotage. Vers Steinmühle.

The "Extern Stones"

Situated not far from the Teutoburg Forest in Westphalia, the "Extern Stones" are a curious, weather-worn mass of sandstone with a unique rock chapel, built on the site of a heathen place of worship. The chapel dates to 1115 A. D.

Les «Externsteine»

Ces étranges rochers déchiquetés, aux abords de la forêt Teutberg en Westphalie, abritent une petite chapelle vétuste datant de 1115, sise à l'endroit même où se célébraient des cultes payens avant la christiani-sation de cette région.

Farmhouse in Oldenburg

This "Ammerland Farmhouse" in Bad Zwischenahn, characterized by its brick and timber construction and its cozy, thatched roof, is one of the most beautiful examples of rural architecture in Germany.

Maison de paysan en Oldenbourg

L'ensemble briques — colombage — toit de roseau: «l'Ammerländer Bauernhaus», à Bad Zwischenahn, représente l'une des réalisations les plus belles de l'architecture rustique en Allemagne.

The Hanseatic city of Bremen

The key in the city's coat of arms indicates that it is the gateway to the world. Typical architectural features are the brick façades of houses along the Weser, the towers of St. Martin, and the cathedral.

Ville Hanséatique de Brême

Le caractère hanséatique se reflète de façon frappante dans les façades de briques, aux fenêtres blanches, des maisons au bord de la Weser, et dans les tours de Saint-Martin et de la cathédrale.

The Town-Hall in Bremen

The Renaissance façade (1608-12) of the old town-hall at Bremen represents the opulence, the 30-foot-high statue of Roland (1404) symbolizes the glory, of this mighty Hanseatic city. Bremen today has a population of 600,000.

L'hôtel de ville à Brême

Cet édifice vénérable, avec son frontispice Renaissance (1608-1612), représente la richesse; et le Roland (1404), haut de 9 m, la fierté civique de cette ville hanséatique qui compte actuellement 600.000 habitants.

Neuharlingersiel

This peaceful seaport in Eastern Frisia is one of numerous small towns on the North Sea coast between Emden and Wilhelmshaven which are almost Dutch in appearance and character.

Neuharlingersiel

Dans la Frise orientale, Neuharlingersiel est un de ces charmants petits villages côtiers, entre Wilhelmshaven et Emden, qui rappellent déjà la Hollande avoisinante.

Heligoland

This island which Germany acquired from Great Britain in 1890, juts up raggedly from the North Sea, about 40 miles northwest of the mouth of the Elbe River. Although extensively damaged during and after World War II, the island is now again a favorite tourist spot.

Helgoland

L'île surgit, en rocher pittoresque, de la mer du Nord, à 65 kilomètres environ de l'embouchure de l'Elbe. Après les destructions de la guerre et de l'après-guerre, l'île est redevenue un lieu très recherché de villégiature pour nombre de visiteurs.

On the North Sea coast

This scene was photographed on the west coast of Schleswig-Holstein, near the seaside resort town of St. Peter-Ording, just as three fishing boats make ready to put to sea. The pale colors are characteristic of the shore belt region in this part of Germany.

Sur la côte de la mer du Nord

Vue maritime prise dans le Slesvig-Holstein, près de St. Peter-Ording: des bateaux de pêche avant le départ, dans ce paysage typique du Nord, aux tendres couleurs.

Nordstrand

Formerly an island, Nordstrand lies off the coast of Holstein to which it is connected by a dam. Numerous small islands near the German North Sea coast, among them the so-called Halligen islets, are remnants of fertile land which was submerged by immense flood storms in former centuries.

Nordstrand

Une image caractéristique de la côte holsteinoise. De nombreux îlots s'échelonnent le long de la côte allemande de la mer du Nord, dont les «Halligen»: restes de la terre ferme engloutie par les marées hautes.

On the Island of Sylt

The largest of the German North Sea islands, Sylt is connected to the mainland by a long dam built in 1925. Its southern part is marked by vast dunes, in the north, the "Red Cliff" (our picture) rises 100 feet above the beach.

L'île de Sylt

Sylt, la plus grande île allemande de la mer du Nord, communique avec la terre ferme par une chaussée construite en 1925. Elle offre un vaste panorama de dunes vers le Sud tandis qu'au Nord s'élève un rocher rouge-jaunâtre «Rotes Kliff» (notre photo) qui atteint 30 m de hauteur.

Glücksburg Castle

A moated castle near Flensburg, close to the Danish border, Glücksburg is the cradle of the royal families of Denmark, Norway and Greece. It was erected on the site of a former monastery between the years 1583 and 1587.

Le Château de Glucksbourg

Berceau des familles royales du Danemark, de Norvège et de Grèce, Glucksbourg est un «château d'eau» des environs de Flensbourg, non loin de la frontière danoise. Il fut construit en 1583-1587, sur l'emplacement d'une abbaye.

Lübeck

The Holstentor (one of the city's old gates), built in 1477, is a proud monument of north German brick Gothic architecture of which this old Hanseatic city has excellent examples. Left, old salt warehouses (16th-18th centuries).

Lubeck

Le «Holstentor» (1477), fier monument de l'art gothique, est un vivant témoignage de cette époque caractérisée, en Allemagne du Nord, par l'emploi de briques. La vieille ville hanséatique en conserve des exemples remarquables. A gauche, de vieux greniers à sel (XVIe-XVIIIe s.).

Farmhouses near Hamburg

These are farmhouses in the „Altes Land", a rich horticultural region west of Hamburg. Elaborately ornamented, brick and half-timbered houses lend the villages here a colorful, lively appearance.

Aux alentours de Hambourg

Ces fermes se trouvent dans le «Vieux Land», une riche région d'arbres fruitiers à l'ouest de Hambourg. Briques et colombage, richement assemblés, rehaussent l'architecture des maisons.

Hamburg

Towers and spires form the silhouette of the city, seen here over the Aussenalster, a wide lake created by a tributary to the Elbe. Hamburg, with 1,800,000 population, is Germany's second largest city.

Hambourg

Tours et clochers caractérisent la silhouette de Hambourg, qui, avec ses 1.800.000 habitants, est la deuxième ville d'Allemagne (après Berlin). Ci-contre vue de la ville; au premier plan, l'Aussenalster, lac formé par un affluent de l'Elbe.

HAMBURG HARBOR, with its
36 miles of piers and covering
an area of 40 square miles,
makes an impressive sight
at night.

LE PORT DE HAMBOURG, avec une
surface de 100 km² et de
60 km de quais, offre,
la nuit, un tableau imposant.

Lüneburg

The old salt town, achieved its greatest importance in the 15th and 16th centuries. The old houses along the River Ilmenau which flows through the town, date back to this time.

Lunebourg

La vieille ville de salines de Lunebourg était à son apogée aux XVe et XVIe siècles. C'est de cette époque que datent aussi les vieilles maisons au bord de l'Ilmenau, rivière qui traverse la ville.

The Lüneburg Heath

Birch trees and heather, juniper and ancient sheep-folds mark the melancholy mood of this largest German heath. It is situated between Hamburg and Hanover, with the picturesque city of Lüneburg at its north-east border.

Les bruyères de Lunebourg

Bouleaux, bruyères, genévriers, ainsi que vieilles bergeries, relèvent la beauté mélancolique de ces landes les plus étendues d'Allemagne, entre Hambourg et Hanovre.

Hanover, Industrial Fairgrounds

Exhibitors representing the international world of industry and technical products from around the globe meet each year at the "Hanover Fair" in the capital of Lower Saxony. Shown here is an open-air display of machinery.

La Foire de Hanovre

Chaque année, les industriels du monde entier se rencontrent dans la capitale de la Basse-Saxe, à l'occasion de la «Foire de Hanovre». Vue sur une exposition de machines, en plein air.

Brunswick

The cathedral, the castle and the statue of the lion were erected in this ducal city of Lower Saxony during the 12th century by Henry the Lion, one of the most powerful of the medieval princes.

Brunsvick

La cathédrale, le château, et le Lion, forment cet ensemble monumental que le Duc Henri le Lion édifia au XIIe siècle ; il était l'un des princes les plus puissants du moyen âge.

The Harz Mountains

The granite cliffs in the Oker Valley are typical of this region which, in former times, was a major German mining center. The Iron Curtain that divides Germany today runs through the center of this mountainous area near the town of Goslar.

Le massif Harz

D'étranges rochers de granit, caractéristiques de la vallée de l'Oker, émergent des collines boisées. Le rideau de fer qui sépare l'Allemagne d'aujourd'hui en deux parties, passe à travers ces montagnes.

Quedlinburg

This picturesque old town in the foothills of the Harz Mountains was a favorite residence of the German emperors. Its collegiate church was built between 997 and 1129 and is the burial place of Henry the Fowler who became King in 919 and died in 936.

Quedlinbourg

La «Frauen-Stiftskirche», construite en 997-1129, marque une époque où cette ville, dans le Harz, était la résidence préférée des empereurs d'Allemagne. L'église renferme le tombeau de Henri Ier (919-936).

Schiller House in Weimar

Friedrich Schiller, the famous German poet and dramatist, lived in this house from 1802 until his death in 1805. During that period Weimar, through Goethe's influence, was the center of German classicism.

Weimar. La maison de Schiller

Cette maison fut habitée par le poète Friedrich Schiller pendant les années 1802-1805, à une époque où la petite ville était le centre littéraire de l'Allemagne, sous l'influence de Goethe.

The Wartburg

Wartburg Fortress near Eisenach, the most famous castle in Thuringia, is linked with the saga of Tannhäuser and the legend of St. Elizabeth. It is best known as the place where Martin Luther took refuge in the 16th century (1521-1522), while working on his translation of the Bible.

La Wartbourg

Près d'Eisenach, la Wartbourg, le château le plus en renom de la Thuringe, est associée aux légendes de Tannhäuser et de Sainte Elisabeth (XIIIe siècle). Connu également par le «concours des ménestrels», ce château fut, au XVIe siècle, le refuge de Martin Luther.

Naumburg

The statue of Uta, from a series of life-sized sculptures in the west choir of the 13th century Romanesque cathedral, is a masterpiece by a medieval German sculptor, called the "Master of Naumburg". Naumburg is situated on the Saale River, not far from Leipzig.

Naumbourg

La statue d'Uta appartient à un cycle de sculptures de grandeur naturelle, dans le chœur ouest de la cathédrale (XIIIe s.). L'artiste anonyme est surnommé le «Maître de Naumbourg».

173

Dresden

With its magnificent Baroque architecture, Dresden was one of Germany's most beautiful cities until it was destroyed in several air raids in 1945. The Zwinger, built by Daniel Pöppelmann in the 18th century for Augustus, King of Poland and Elector of Saxony, was recently reconstructed. In the picture: the "Kronentor" (Crown Gate).

Dresde

Jusqu'à sa destruction en 1945, Dresde était l'une des plus belles villes allemandes, surtout pour son baroque. Le «Zwinger» (sur la photo: porte de la couronne), édifié au XVIIIe s. par Daniel Pöppelmann, pour l'électeur Auguste le Fort, a été refait ces dernières années.

Saxonian Switzerland

These massive rock formations, called the "Bastei", or Bastion, are part of the Elbe Sandstone Mountains, popularly called "Saxonian Switzerland", south of Dresden. In the background, Mount Lilienstein.

Suisse saxonne

Le massif gréseux au sud de Dresde, appelé familièrement «Suisse saxonne», compte parmi les plus intéressantes de ses bizarres formations rocheuses le lieudit «Bastei», ou «la Bastille». A l'arrière-plan le mont Lilienstein.

Berlin

The Kurfürstendamm is the liveliest and most popular boulevard in the western part of the divided city. In the background is the ruin of the "Kaiser-Wilhelm-Gedächtniskirche", flanked by a modern annex and bell tower, designed by Prof. Eiermann. Just a few miles away lies the infamous Berlin Wall that cuts Germany's largest city in two.

Berlin

Le «Kurfürstendamm» est l'avenue la plus connue et la plus animée de la partie Ouest de la métropole. A l'arrière-plan, on voit les ruines de la «Kaiser-Wilhelm-Gedächtniskirche» avec ses annexes modernes. Le mur qui maintenant coupe en deux la plus grande ville de l'Allemagne, ne se trouve qu'à quelques kilomètres.

Potsdam

The buildings erected here by Frederick the Great, King of Prussia and friend of Voltaire, are a rare document of the cultivated spirit that reigned in Prussia during the 18th century. The concert room of the New Palace was built around 1767.

Potsdam

Les édifices que fit bâtir Frédéric II le Grand, roi de Prusse, ami et hôte de Voltaire, sont des témoignages exquis d'un esprit raffiné. La salle de concert, au Nouveau Palais, date d'environ 1767.

Neubrandenburg

The Treptow Gate in this little town in Mecklenburg is a masterpiece of north German brick Gothic that decorated churches and public buildings in this region in the 14th and 15th centuries.

Neubrandenbourg

La porte de Treptow, dans la petite ville mecklembourgeoise, est un chef-d'œuvre de l'art gothique caractérisé par l'emploi de briques en Allemagne du Nord. Ce style est celui de nombreux édifices profanes et sacrés, construits aux XIVe et XVe siècles.

Rügen

The Baltic region reaches a high point of scenic beauty in Rügen, the largest of the German islands. White chalk cliffs, crowned by forests of beech trees, rise several hundred feet above the water.

Rügen

La plus grande île allemande, Rügen, est l'un des plus beaux sites tout autour de la mer Baltique. Des rochers crétacés de plus de 100 m, blancs comme la neige, s'élancent au milieu de forêts de hêtres.

The publisher wishes to thank the photographers listed below whose contributions made this book possible.
The figures indicate the page numbers of the illustrations

Toni Schneiders, Lindau-Bad Schachen: 14, 18/19, 20, 32, 35, 39, 40, 47, 48, 59, 72/73, 97, 98, 130.
Toni Schneiders (Archiv-Kinkelin, Frankfurt): 156.
Heinz Müller-Brunke, Grassau: 10, 56, 78, 82, 101, 109, 114, 129, 164, front cover.
C. L. Schmitt, Munich, 13, 23, 43, 86, 94, 142, 146, 150, 159.
Hans Hartz, Hamburg: 27, 67, 105, 141, 153, 154/155.
Umschau, Frankfurt: 175, 176, 180, 183, 184.
Gerhard Klammet, Ohlstadt: 64, 71, 90, 133, 163.
Peter Keetman, Breitbrunn: 9, 24, back cover.
Bertram Luftbild, Munich: 28, 31.
Klaus Beyer, Weimar: 167, 171.
Dr. Harald Busch, Frankfurt: 106, 113.
Cramers Kunstanstalt, Dortmund: 121.
Rudolf Dodenhoff, Worpswede: 134.
Dieter Geissler, Stuttgart: 51, 52.
Hans Huber, Garmisch-Partenkirchen: 17, 63.
Lossen-Foto, Heidelberg: 85, 102.
Aero-Lux, Frankfurt: 110, 122.
Studio Bartcky, Frankfurt: 172.
Dr. Hell-Bavaria, Gauting near Munich: 93.

Höch-Bavaria, Gauting near Munich: 68.
Bleicke Bleicken, Kampen, Sylt: 145.
Hans Breidenstein, Frankfurt: 77.
Harry Evers, Mainz: 168.
Leif Geiges, Freiburg in the Breisgau: 44.
Leo Gundermann, Würzburg: 74.
Foto-Hauck Werbestudio, Mannheim: 89.
Heinz Herfort, Kempten: 60.
Lothar Kaster, Gruiten: 117.
Pressebilderdienst Klaus Kindermann & Co., Berlin-Wilmersdorf: 179.
Rüdiger Kluge, Pinneberg: 160.
Deutsche Luftbild KG., Hamburg: 138.
Erich Müller, Kassel: 55.
Preiss & Co. (Braun), Ismaning: 125.
Presse-Foto Seeger, Ebingen: 36.
Hans Retzlaff, Tann in the Rhön: 81.
Schöning & Co., Lübeck: 149.
Ludwig Schumacher, Emden: 137.
Dieter Storp, Düsseldorf: 118.
Hans Wagner, Vlotho: 126.